Helen Orme is a successful author of fiction and non-fiction, particularly for reluctant and struggling readers. She has written over fifty books for Ransom Publishing.

Helen was a teacher for nearly thirty years. She worked as a Special Educational Needs Co-ordinator in a large comprehensive school, as an advisory teacher for IT and as teacher-in-charge for a pupil referral unit. These experiences have been invaluable in her writing.

StreetWise

The Best Thing Ever
gambling, rebelling against parents

Speed
getting involved in crime

The Newcomer
outsiders, racism, intolerance

I Dare You
taking risks

Fixed It!
cyberbullying

I Can't Help It
smoking

Best Mates
coping with peer pressure

Everyone Does It
cheating

Just Try It!
drugs

Don't Believe Her
sex

Just One More
alcohol

Taking Responsibility
conflicting priorities: home and school

I Can't Help It

Helen Orme

Ransom

HULL LIBRARIES	
102282047	
Bertrams	02/07/2014
	£6.99

Street**Wise**

I Can't Help It
by Helen Orme

Published by Ransom Publishing Ltd.
Radley House, 8 St. Cross Road, Winchester, Hampshire SO23 9HX, UK
www.ransom.co.uk

ISBN   978 184167 344 8
First published in 2014

Copyright © 2014 Ransom Publishing Ltd.
Text copyright © 2014 Helen Orme
Cover photograph copyright © sandsun.

A CIP catalogue record of this book is available from the British Library.

All rights reserved. No part of this publication may be reproduced, stored in a retrieval system, or transmitted, in any form or by any means, electronic, mechanical, photocopying, recording or otherwise, without the prior permission of the publishers.

The right of Helen Orme to be identified as the author of this Work has been asserted by her in accordance with sections 77 and 78 of the Copyright, Design and Patents Act 1988.

CONTENTS

1	Horrible	7
2	Leave Dad Alone!	10
3	The Worst Thing	15
4	'You Could Have Died'	19
5	'It's My Fault'	24
	Questions on the Story	27
	Discussion Points	30
	Activities	33

ONE

Horrible

Amy didn't want to go home. But she couldn't put it off any longer.

She hoped Dad wasn't in yet. It was much worse when he was at home.

*****

She went round to the back door and pushed it open.

'Hello love, did you have a good day?'

Good. Mum was in and Dad hadn't got back yet.

She gave her mum a hug.

'Not bad. When's tea?'

'When Dad gets in. About an hour.'

'I'm going up to do some work on the computer then,' she said.

It was always better when she could escape to her room.

*****

Amy was well into her homework when she heard the door slam.

She sighed. Now she'd have to go back downstairs.

It would be horrible; she just knew it.

TWO

Leave Dad Alone!

Mum called to her. She took a deep breath and opened her door.

Downstairs in the kitchen the table was set for tea. There was a nice smell of food, but she felt like choking as she went in.

'Dad,' she said. 'We're just going to eat. Couldn't you wait even a little while?'

'Don't start,' he said.

But he smiled at her as he said it. He knew how she felt and didn't want to upset her.

'I can't smoke in work these days, you know that. At least I can still have a cig in my own home.'

'But … '

'Stop it,' said Mum sharply. 'Leave Dad alone. He's had a hard day.'

Amy sighed again and sat down to eat.

*****

She thought about all the things she could say. She said them often enough, but Dad always had an answer.

'It's bad for you.'

'My dad smoked from the age of 14

and it never did him any harm.'

'The whole house smells.'

'Your mum always uses air freshener.'

'I can't breathe.'

'Well, open the window in your room.'

THREE

The Worst Thing

It was true, though.

Sometimes she felt as though she couldn't get enough air. It made her feel sick and her chest hurt.

And she worried about them. They

both smoked, but Dad was the worst. He'd always got a cigarette going, even in the car.

She'd done all the smoking things at school. She'd seen the films about lung cancer and stuff, and the pictures of lungs.

She'd tried to tell Dad, but he wouldn't listen.

*****

The worst thing was the smell. It got on everything.

Air freshener didn't make any difference. Even opening her bedroom window didn't help much.

And her friends noticed the smell on her clothes. Her best friends knew it wasn't her, but other people thought that she smoked.

*****

And there was Dave!

She really fancied Dave. She thought he liked her too.

In the end, Jas, her best friend, had asked him. Jas didn't want to tell Amy what he'd said, but Amy made her.

'She looks cute, but no way will I go out with her while she smells like that. Tell her to give up, then I might.'

FOUR
'You Could Have Died'

Monday morning.

Amy didn't feel well, but not bad enough to stay home.

Anyway, she knew that staying at home would make her feel worse.

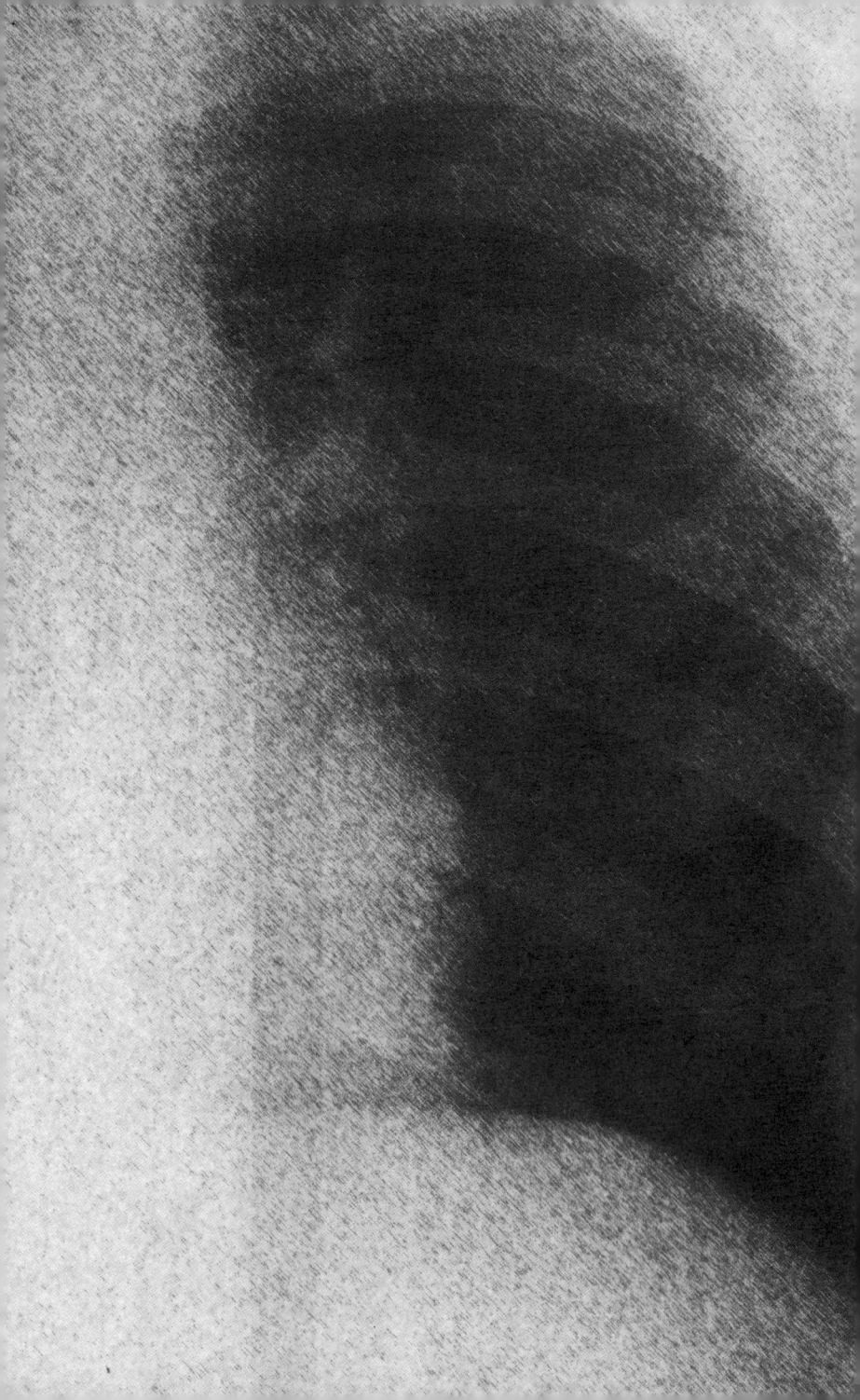

During the morning, Amy began to feel really bad. She kept coughing and wheezing. Her face was all sweaty.

It happened during double Science.

There was a funny smell in the lab. Amy couldn't breathe. The pain in her chest was horrible. She was choking, gasping for air.

She wanted to cry out, but she couldn't …

*****

'You're a lucky girl,' the doctor said. 'It was a severe asthma attack. If your Science teacher hadn't known what to do, it could have been very serious. You could have died.'

Mum and Dad were sitting round the hospital bed, looking frightened.

'But Amy's never had asthma,' Mum said. 'Why has it happened now?'

'Many things can trigger it,' said the doctor.

'May I ask, do either of you smoke?'

FIVE
'It's My Fault'

The next day, Amy was able to go home.

It smelt really different. Mum had been washing and cleaning, and all the stale smoky smells had gone.

'I've given up,' Mum said. 'I had no

idea what it was doing to you!'

'Where's Dad?'

'Not sure – in the garden, I think.'

Amy found him at the bottom of the garden – smoking.

And he was crying.

Amy was shocked. She had never seen her dad cry before.

'What's the matter, Dad?'

Dad threw down the cigarette and

gave Amy a hug.

'Amy, I feel so bad. You could have died. And it's my fault.'

Amy hated to see her dad like this.

'Dad, just give it up. Then everything will be fine.'

'That's the problem, Amy. I've tried. Lots of times.

'But I just can't.'

Questions on the Story

- Why didn't Amy want to go home?

- Why wouldn't Dave go out with her?

◆ What did Amy's parents do afterwards?

Discussion Points

- Should tobacco be made an illegal drug?

- If not, should people be allowed to smoke in their own home?

- Amy's dad knew what smoking could do. And yet he still smoked.

  Why?

Activities

◆ Write the script for a TV advert to encourage people to give up smoking.

- Some people think that smoking in cars should be banned.

  In groups, debate the arguments for and against.

- ◆ Design a cigarette packet that will put people off smoking.